Our Love and a Smile

by Hattie Dumeraf
Edited by Mike Fairchild and Myron Bruce

© 2025 Spiritbuilding Publishers.
All rights reserved. No part of this book may be reproduced in any form without the written permission of the publisher.

Published by
Spiritbuilding Publishers
9700 Ferry Road, Waynesville, Ohio 45068

OUR LOVE AND A SMILE
By Hattie Dumeraf

ISBN: 978-1-964-80552-8

Spiritbuilding
PUBLISHERS

spiritbuilding.com

Introduction

It's a beautiful Sunday morning as we walk into the foyer, ready to worship! You recall the words of David as he penned Psalm 122, *"I was glad when they said, 'Let us go to the house of the Lord.' … "* You have come with other believers eager to rekindle a heart of fellowship and reconnect relationships with brothers and sisters in the kingdom. It's the beginning of our time together, a start to the day of worship.

For most of us, one of the first faces we meet as we come into the building on Sunday morning is the friendly smile from one that we know as "the Greeter." An individual who has volunteered to get up early and welcome each person who walks into the foyer. It's true, some congregations struggle with getting a 'team' of greeters in place, and yet there are some blessed with four or more greeters who stand ready to spread Christian friendliness. Developing a rapport with visitors and supporting the membership is something to be desired.

For those who stand up on any given Sunday to spread love to the families who visit your congregations, this book is for you! This is a compilation of six years of handwritten poetry by a beautiful soul who was in her late 80s. Hattie Dumerauf spent her final years of life as a member of the Waterview church of Christ in Richardson, Texas. Her ministry of encouragement came in the form of letters and poems that she wrote by hand every Sunday, specifically for those she affectionately referred to as "the Smile Greeters." Hattie was unable to drive herself on Sunday, so her dear friend, Mike Fairchild, picked her up each Sunday morning for worship services. This ministry from Mike, coupled with Hattie's words of encouragement, has provided a work to touch lives across the years. Though Hattie passed in 2012, a memorial can be found in the book, *The Splendor of Worship (A Much Better Place)* that honors her memory and embraces her heart of encouragement.

Greeters, "Smile Greeters," as you read this book, I hope you will take to heart how much you are needed in the Lord's church. You, greeters, provide a warm smile that welcomes the weary heart. You offer a friendly wave that greets the family of God who is seeking encouragement in His church. You stand as the first tier to welcome those visiting your assembly. And you can help set the stage for many who have come to fellowship and worship! So, I pray this book, assembled from the heart of a beautiful sister in Christ, will not only encourage you but will be a support to you and your ministry. Thank you for your smile, your welcoming wave, and your enduring words of compassion for God's people.

A Word to Sunday Morning Greeters ... from Hattie

*"You get no prize or medal for what you do,
but how good it must make you feel.*

*For that Smile you give a share of God's love that is so uplifting and real.
Your Smile is an open umbrella that shields us from life's troubled storm.
And on a summer's day, it's a ray of sunshine to us, sheltered and warm.
But most of all, your Smile is like a blessed message from Heaven above.
A light that shines from your heart, declaring to all that God is love."*

—Hattie D. & Nina

Foreword: Mike Fairchild

When Myron asked if I would write the foreword to this book of Hattie's poetry, I told him I would consider it an honor. And it is!

During a person's life, many individuals come and go. Some of these people leave a lasting, positive impression, and in my life, Hattie Dumerauf was one of those special people. I will always admire and remember her.

One day, I received a phone call from the office at the Waterview church of Christ. I had no way of knowing that this phone call would change my life forever. One of our ministers, Dub Harrison, asked if I would consider providing transportation to church for a lady who had recently moved to Richardson, Texas, from Davenport, Iowa. I agreed to help, and that was the start of a ten-year relationship with Hattie. Every Sunday, we traveled down Waterview Drive, and the conversation always centered around the majesty of God and how much He had blessed Hattie during the week. I could tell after our first trip to church how blessed I would be by knowing this sweet lady from Davenport, Iowa.

While Hattie had no material possessions, she had the spirit of God in her heart, and she shared it with me. Knowing her made me a better man and helped me to see what was really important in life. This too, you will see, you will read, as you turn the pages of her book.

As I would drive up to the place where she rented a room, there she would be, standing on the front porch, waving with a big smile on her face. She was there rain or shine waiting on me to take her to her favorite place on earth, the Waterview church of Christ. That is how our Sunday mornings started each week. I will always thank God that I was the fortunate one to get the phone call that brought Hattie into my life.

Later, we would add another lady to our Sunday morning trip down Waterview Drive, Nina Small. Nina, though 'small' in stature, had the same love for the Lord that Hattie did. For several years, we enjoyed so many good times on our way to church. Unfortunately, Nina was injured in an accident in her home and was not able to go with us any longer.

Each Sunday, Hattie would distribute her handwritten poetry to various members at church. She looked at this as her ministry! The poems in this book are some of the ones that she gave me over the years. I cherish each one of them as I hear Hattie's voice each time I read them.

God blesses each of us in so many ways, and He truly blessed me by allowing me to part of Hattie's life.

Dedications

To stop for a moment and say 'thank you' to those who were significant in the influence of the collection of these verses would be a difficult task. There are so many who should be recognized for the inspiration of this publication, but rest assured that if it weren't for the thoughtfulness and attentiveness of Hattie as she penned these words of cheer week after week, we wouldn't have this book. And of course, as you will come to know, the Sunday morning "Smile Greeters" (as Hattie so affectionately referenced) were the first to receive these personal, handwritten notes. To list each of these greeters would be next to impossible. And I would be amiss with this moment of dedication if I failed to mention a group of women at the Waterview church of Christ who formulated the plan to have a team of greeters who would welcome our guests. The result was the origination of a program we called the "Heart to Heart Greeters." To each of those unnamed women with a mind to welcome and to the Waterview elders and ministers who supported and encouraged the idea … to you this book is dedicated. You all foresaw a need to extend a loving hand to those who would attend Sunday morning worship services. Members and guests alike, to this day, receive a warm welcome because of the thoughtfulness and the leadership you all provided!

And that leads me to yet one more dedication that you must consider. To ignore this individual would be, at the least, a lapse in judgment. If you read the forward to this book, you, in essence, have met him … Mike Fairchild. It is to him that this book is also dedicated. His faithful example to bring Hattie and Nina to church on Sunday morning demonstrated his selfless attitude and his giving heart. Mike is the one who inspired this document, as he cared for two aging women who needed a Christian friend. He understood and demonstrated the words of Christ in Matthew 25:35. To those on the right, Jesus said, *"I was a stranger, and you invited me in."* Not only did Mike welcome the stranger, but he also *"visited the widows in distress."* James 1:27, *"Pure and undefiled religion in the sight of our God is this: to visit the orphans and widows in their distress, and to keep oneself unstained by the world."* Over the years, hundreds of poems were written by Hattie Dumerauf, and Sunday after Sunday, Mike Fairchild collected them. This book includes only a fraction of those stanzas. Many now serve as the foundation of this book. But it was the dedicated heart of my dear friend Mike Fairchild that led me to publish the words of one beautiful Christian woman's love.

Whether you know these individuals or not, these servants in the Lord's church are an example that should be preserved through the years. They were the masterminds behind the formation of the Waterview church of Christ's Sunday morning Greeters, the 'Smile Greeters.' If you, like they, have given yourself to welcome the Sunday morning visitor, you too deserve more than just a 'thank you.' May your years of service be a beacon of light across your community and within your congregation. Let these poems inspire you to reach others with a welcome smile, an outstretched hand of love, and a glowing heart of Christian fellowship.

1-11-09

A New Year lies before us what it will hold we don't know its true.

So lets keep the light of Faith with in us the Holy Spirit will guide us through

And lets keep Gods Banner before us it will be a Shield from evils and harms.

If we should get weary and stumble He will be there to lift us with Loving arms

Never lose the desire to be Faithful in Prayer for the Soul of your fellow man

This shows the Lord You follow His Word and you are true to His Plan.

Lets begin this New Year with the knowledge we are Gods People Sanctified and free.

So Glory to the Father, Glory to the Son Glory to the Holy Spirit as it was, as it is and forever shall be.

The Waterview Church Smile Greeters face the New Year to with Gods Love in their Smile.

Telling all "Come on in God will make your time worthwhile.

Our Love and a Smile
Hattie D & Nina

A New Year

Week 1—January 11, 2009

A New Year lies before us, what it will hold we don't know, it's true.

So, let's keep the light of Faith within us, the Holy Spirit will guide us through.
And let's keep God's Banner before us, it will be a Shield from evils and harms.
If we should get weary and stumble, He will be there to lift us with Loving arms.
Never lose the desire to be Faithful in Prayer for the Soul of your fellow man.
This shows the Lord you follow His Word, and you are true to His Plan.
Let's begin this New Year with the knowledge we are God's People, Sanctified and free.
So, Glory to the Father, Glory to the Son, Glory to the Holy Spirit as it was, as it is, and forever shall be.
The Smile Greeters face the New Year too with God's Love in their Smile.
Telling all 'Come on in, God will make your time worthwhile.'

Our Love and a Smile ... Hattie D. & Nina

Four Tators

Week 2—January 17, 2010

There are numerous vegetables in the World, but I've narrowed it down to four.

They are only ordinary Tators, but each has their own personality and more.

First, we have the Agitators who try to stir up trouble wherever they go. They have no regard for Rules or Laws, but their 'know it all' manner they Love to show.

Next, we have the Hesitators who always question what they should do. Their church truly needs their aid, but they could use a new car, too.

Now we have the Commentators who always have plenty to say. He tries to steer the conversation to where he comes out top man of the day.

Last but not least is the old Sweet tator, he Lives every day to help his Friends. He strives to follow God's Plan of Love, and his quest never ends.

We are greeted by the Smile Greeters every Sunday, passing on God's Love so true.

As we enter in, let's think and ponder which Tator applies to you?

Our Love and a Smile … Hattie D. & Nina

A Dismal World Without a Smile

Week 3—January 25, 2009

Wouldn't this be a dismal World if no one ever Smiled at you?

It would be like a dark cloud between Heaven and Earth where God's Love couldn't shine through.

But God said, 'No, that can never be … ' so He gave everyone a Beautiful Smile.

A frown on the face is out of date; a Loving Smile is more in style.

So He gave the Smile Greeters a very important place.

At the Door of the Church, God's Love shining on their face.

So show you're in style by that Loving Smile that God lives in your Heart.

For the World needs that Love from God to know in that Love they are a part.

Don't ever get too busy you don't have time to talk to God for a while,

And you will find you are facing all of Life's problems with a Smile.

Our Love and a Smile … Hattie D. & Nina

Contrasts in Life

Week 4—January 31, 2010

For every sunset, there's a sunrise, for every Winter, there's a Spring.
For every word in anger spoken, there's joy and gladness, kind words bring.
For every raindrop, there's a sunbeam. For every tear, a Loving Smile.
For every storm, a Promise given, this too shall pass in just a while.
Life's made of contrasts, sweet and bitter, and into each Life both must fall.
But be it a trial or be it a Blessing, we know God's hand is in it all.
If Life were always bright and Happy, would we then seek help from above?
Or know the joy when morning breaks with Rainbowed skies of Hope and Love?
The Smile Greeters show God's love in the Smile upon their face.
That shows you God is here; you have come to the right place.

Our Love and a Smile ... Hattie D. & Nina

2-4-07

Does God ever give a Smile to His Dear Ones yes indeed He does He doesn't keep them He gives them away.

He gave one to the Waterview Church Smile Greeters to greet everyone each Holy Day.

What each one of us does with that Smile is up to us but think of the Joy it may bring.

It may find a Heart thats heavy laden and lift that Heart to sing.

So lets do as God gives us an example to do take that Loving Smile and give it away.

That will eliminate someones rain clouds and give them a Rainbow Day.
    Our Love and a Smile ☺
      Hattie D + Nina

God's Smile

Week 1—February 4, 2007

Does God ever give a Smile to His Dear Ones … "Yes, indeed He does."
*   He doesn't keep them; He gives them away.*
He gave one to the Smile Greeters to greet everyone each Holy Day.
What each one of us does with that Smile is up to us, but think of the Joy it
*   may bring.*
It may find a Heart that's heavy laden and lift that Heart to sing.
So, let's do as God gives us an example to do, take that Loving Smile and
*   give it away.*
That will eliminate someone's rain clouds and give them a Rainbow Day.

*   Our Love and a Smile … Hattie D. & Nina*

St. Valentine's Day

Week 2—February 14, 2010

We celebrate a day of Love today. We call it St. Valentine's Day.
But our God, who placed that Love in our Hearts, says, 'Don't keep it, give it away.'
So spread that Love like Sunshine, embrace the Loved ones that are sad.
Give your Love, give them joy, those actions will leave them feeling glad.
It's alright to say, 'I Love you' to someone every day.
To obey our God's Command in a warm and Loving way.
The World is full of sorrows that sometimes touch us all.
And to know that we are Loved lifts us up whenever we fall.
Love is the Rainbow after the storm, or like roses on a Summer's day.
It's a Smile that lightens a time of darkness and chases all fears away.
Three little words can mean so much, and they are not hard to say.
It's alright to say I Love You to a Loved one every day.
The Smile Greeters stand ready to give Love too.
For from their Hearts they give those three Blessed words, God Loves You.

Our Love and a Smile … Hattie D. & Nina

Wrapped in Love

Week 3—February 18, 2007

A Smile is a kindness wrapped in Love. Did you give one of yours today?
That Smile will light up a cloudy day and chase dark clouds away.
If we all would take the time to give a Smile to someone in place of a frown
…
We could all help the World be a better place with God's approval
  Smiling down.
Today, there may be tears in your Heart, but there's also a Smile living
  there …
For the Smile Greeters gave one of God's Loving Smiles to share.
So if you give someone the gift of your Smile, feel content you did your part,
To bring a ray of Sunshine, Love that will grow in someone's Heart.

Our Love and a Smile … Hattie D. & Nina

Do We Need the Snow?

Week 4—February 28, 2010

Down it came, soft feathers of white like a blanket covering the ground.
Snowflakes like a ballet of beauty, silent dancers not making a sound.
It kept falling down getting deeper and deeper. I thought, 'When will it cease?'
I knew there was no way I could make it stop, soon it was up to my knees.
Who needs snow, I grumbled to myself; it's a trouble and nuisance too.
All of a sudden, I heard the soft voice of the Lord saying, 'Who needs this snow? You do.'
Without rain or snow, what would the Farmers do without any moisture in the soil?
The seeds that were sown couldn't push through dry ground, so their labor would be a futile toil.
So, the next time it snows, don't whine or complain, just accept the snowy day.
Get out the old snow shovel, put a Smile on your face, and shovel, shovel away.
The Smile Greeters respect those snow showers, too.
Their Smiles will melt the snow from your path and let God's Love shine through.

Our Love and a Smile … Hattie D. & Nina

3-7-10

What a terrible dream I had last night America was shutting down.

They were locking doors shutting out lights all over town to town!

Industries had moved away there was no work to be had anywhere.

Some Foreign Nation had purchased our wonderful Home Land share by share

I thought how could this possibly happen to the greatest Country in the Universe!

It was sold to the highest bidder to the holder of the winners purse.

I awoke from my dream shouting "You cant take this Land from me".

Its a God Loving Country that cant be bought God made it the Land of the Free.

There may be some that would sell her out but my America will ever stand.

For we are a God Loving Nation in His Service ever Proud, Free

A Terrible Dream

Week 1—March 7, 2010

What a terrible dream I had last night, America was shutting down.

They were locking doors, shutting out lights all over, town to town.

Industries had moved away, there was no work to be had anywhere.

Some Foreign Nation had purchased our wonderful Homeland, share by share.

I thought, how could this possibly happen to the greatest Country in the Universe?

It was sold to the highest bidder, to the holder of the winner's purse.

I awoke from my dream shouting, 'You can't take this Land from me.'

It's a God Loving Country that can't be bought; God made it the Land of the Free.

There may be some that would sell her out, but my America will ever stand.

For we are a God Loving Nation, in His Service ever Proud, Free, and Grand.

The Smile Greeters stand at their post Proud of America too.

Proving their Love for God will ever remain ... Loyal and True.

Our Love and a Smile ... Hattie D. & Nina

The Wiley One

Week 2—March 15, 2009

If you are a true believer of God, may He ever keep you in His view.
For you are in the middle of a constant battle between God and you know who.
This 'Who' is a wily creature who is out to catch you in his snare.
There's no distance that's too far for him to go; you can find him anywhere.
He won't go near the Smile Greeters; he is wary of their Smile.
He doesn't care for their Love of our Mighty God; it doesn't suit his wicked style.
He thinks he has Power, but he is a big joke, for he can't get in the Church Door.
The Congregation's Love of God keeps him out, for they have the Power of God in store.
You ask, 'Who is this terror, that threatens us every season, day to day?'
It's old Satan as we know him who thinks he has Power ... but he trembles when we Pray.

Our Love and a Smile ... Hattie D. & Nina

Don't Forget to Pray

Week 3—March 21, 2010

Sometimes we get involved with Life's problems and we forget to Pray.
But God is ever there before you, so you can cope with each new day.
So, I say, 'Lord, please remind me of promises I made in Prayer.'
I said, If you relieve me of the worrisome burdens I bear,
I would always be trusting, and my Faith would never stray.
I would know You walk beside me, every hour of the day.'
But Lord, I'm only human, and should those burdens reappear,
I may forget I promised to trust You without fear.
Again, Lord, please remind me that I made a sacred vow.
To never doubt Your Goodness, Lord, please remind me now.
Don't ever be too busy to talk to Him awhile.
And you will find you are facing each problem with a Smile.
The Smile Greeters show to all on Sunday morn ...
Their Faith and Belief in our Lord by their Loving Smiles that are worn.

Our Love and a Smile ... Hattie D. & Nina

When Winter Holds On

Week 4—March 28, 2010

Old Winter had received his notice, his reign was over, it was time for him to go.

But he is hanging on and won't give up without a final blast of cold weather, rain, and snow.

Spring is waiting down the road to take over and make the Earth fresh and new.

When Spring is in the air, God is there too, with Blessings in what we say and do.

So, goodbye to Winter. Please don't hurry back; we are not sorry to see you go.

God has opened the door so Spring can enter in with a warm Smile and a welcoming hello.

So let's enjoy our Springtime with Rainbowed skies and gentle rain.

For as time goes fleeting by, and before we know it, old Winter will be knocking again.

It matters not the time of year, whether skies of blue or skies of gray.

Each Season is fashioned by our God in His Own Special way.

The Smile Greeters stand with their Smiles bright as the morning Sun.

That Smile is a sign that Spring is coming with Peace and Blessings for everyone.

Our Love and a Smile ... Hattie D. & Nina

Hold on Tight

Week 5—March 27, 2011

The Sun is always shining, although at times it can't be found.
Clouds of depression seem to hide it, where suffering and misery abound.
Some days are dark and dreary, but our Faith can pull us through.
If only we will be patient, the sky will again be blue.
If we but trust and hold on tight and never give in to despair.
Soon we will see a ray of light to let us know it's there.
Yes, we shall see the Sun shine again, and we shall see its radiant glow.
The clouds will always fade away; it is God's Plan, you know.
I believe that our God hears us always, anytime, anywhere.
When the load of Life's troubles are lifted to prove He answers Prayer.
We must be sure to hold out a hand, give a word of Love and a Smile.
To help the Friend beside you walk across each weary mile.
The Smile Greeters believe God's Love is in every part of Life; His Love is
    there to share.
Grab handfuls and then toss them. It's up to us to show we care.

Our Love and a Smile … Hattie D. & Nina

4-5-09

Whenever we get on our feet Life knocks us down once more.
At times we would rather stay in bed afraid of whats in store.
Yet we struggle through our fears stand up each day and fight.
And ask the Lord for patience when we go to sleep at night.
When we get weary from this Life it takes its toll within.
Our work and worries bring us down and soon our Faith wears thin.
The hand of God is still in reach if we can just hold on.
For in the midst of pain and tears the darkness turns to dawn.
Dont let the light begin to fade for Christ still shines in you.
The World will always try to bring you down but God will see us through
The Waterview Church Smile Greeters greet you with Gods Love at the door
And when you enter in you will find Gods Blessings and so much more

When Life's a Struggle

Week 1—April 5, 2009

Whenever we get on our feet, Life knocks us down once more.
At times, we would rather stay in bed, afraid of what's in store.
Yet we struggle through our fears, stand up each day, and fight.
And ask the Lord for patience when we go to sleep at night.
When we get weary from this Life, it takes its toll within.
Our work and worries bring us down, and soon our Faith wears thin.
The hand of God is still in reach, if we can just hold on.
For in the midst of pain and tears, the darkness turns to dawn.
Don't let the light begin to fade, for Christ still shines in you.
The World will always try to bring you down, but God will see us through.
The Smile Greeters greet you with God's Love at the door.
And when you enter in you will find God's Blessings and so much more.

Our Love and a Smile ... Hattie D. & Nina

Week 2—April 12, 2009

Love is like a butterfly; it goes wherever it pleases and pleases wherever it goes.

The Love given to mankind was the Love of Jesus; it was a gift our Savior chose.

That gift of Love was in exchange for His Life that He gave for you and I.

Not just to keep, but to give to Loved ones, to Friends, even strangers passing by.

Love is a power medicine, and given every day, it's healing power never ends.

It warms the Heart and brightens the day in the comforting message it sends.

Let each of us give our Love freely, let Jesus know His sacrifice was not in vain.

Let our butterflies of Love fly away to light on Loved ones again and again.

For that gift of Love was given to us by Jesus to prove He Loved us so.

So let's carry that Banner of Love with us wherever we happen to go.

The Smile Greeters with their Love pass that along,

To show the Lord His Love will ever remain constant and strong.

Our Love and a Smile … Hattie D. & Nina

A Key to God's Storehouse

Week 3—April 13, 2008

The day may be a cloudy one and maybe hold a chance of showers.

But the Smile Greeters are there with their Smiles like beautiful flowers.

Now, a Smile on your face shows that God Lives within, and His Love is shining through.

So just try it once, give someone a Smile and see what they will do.

Did you give someone a Smile today? If you did, you will get one back.

For Smiles are a key to God's Storehouse of Love, and that Love will never lack.

Never leave kind words unspoken, greet each one you meet with a Smile.

For that sign of God's Love lightens many Hearts and makes one feel worthwhile.

God gives us that Loving Smile on our face, but He tells us to give it away.

So look for someone who needs a lift and give them God's gift today.

Our Love and a Smile ... Hattie D. & Nina

Ode to Ministers

Week 4—April 18, 2010

We have so many sorts of holidays we celebrate throughout the year.
Why not hold a Special Thank You for our Minister that we hold very Dear.
He perhaps could have chosen a Profession that would give him wealth and security.
But he chose to teach God's Holy Words that would truly benefit you and me.
So today we take a moment to say how very much we Appreciate you.
For those Words of God you bring to us is Life's Light that will guide us through.
You stand up front so tall and proud for you, Live what you Preach each day.
He lets you know that with your Faith, Life's troubles will never stay.
So hear our voices of appreciation, we have in our Hearts that we all give to you.
May you truly Reap God's Precious Love for the labor of Love that in His Name you do.
Other Houses of Worship cry they are losing members, but may we continue to grow.
For God chooses the right person to do His Work and His Blessed Love to sow.
The Smile Greeters will tell you they are proud of their Minister, too.
They stand proud of their job on Sunday morn, for that's what they were chosen to do.

Our Love and a Smile ... Hattie D. & Nina

A Daily Deed

Week 5—April 26, 2009

If you have a moment with nothing to do, look into the week that's coming to you.

MONDAY—Look for a Smile today and return it with one of your own. It gives someone new Faith and Hope; it's such a beautiful loan.

TUESDAY—Think of a thought that is kind, 'As ye sow, so shall ye reap.' Be sure to pass it along, for they are too precious to keep.

WEDNESDAY—Forget yesterday's old sorrows, mistakes, sadness, and pain. Lift your Heart with Hope and a song as a flower to sun and to rain.

THURSDAY—Offer a word of comfort and a Prayer for a Dear Loved One in need. A thoughtful gift, some flowers, or a Smile can make one feel rich indeed.

FRIDAY—You may not pass this way again, so do any good you can do. Don't put it off till tomorrow; the chance may be lost to you.

SATURDAY—Today may soon be a memory, so don't let it come to an end … without a Smile, without a song, or a Loving word with a Friend.

SUNDAY—Don't let worry or care depress you or brush the day's joy away. But rise and give Thanks to our God for His Love and a Blessed day.

The Smile Greeters follow these words sincere and true.
They greet you with these thoughts every Sunday and pass them on to you.

Our Love and a Smile … Hattie D. & Nina

5-9-10

Today we give Tribute to all Mothers and their boundless Love through the years.

She was always there through times of skinned knees, monsters in the night and there to wipe away tears.

Fathers had to work to keep up a home but a Mother was on call 24 hours a day.

Her wages were based on the Love you gave she performed her duties with little pay.

Children whine and complain but Mothers have Patience to spare.

When her day is unsettled she reaches in her Heart and finds Peace in Gods Love that is there.

She spreads her Love like a blanket covering her Loved ones from want and harm.

When your day holds troubles she gives you shelter in two Loving arms.

Its true that many Dear Mothers are in Heaven but it will be easy to find.

Many signs of that Precious Mothers Love she left for you behind.

So take your Mother in your arms today tell her what she means to you.

That Love she gives you has Blessed your Life for Gods Love is in it to.

The Waterview Church Smile Greeters remember their Mothers Love to.

A Tribute to Mothers

Week 1—May 9, 2010

Today, we give Tribute to all Mothers and their boundless Love through the years.

She was always there through times of skinned knees, monsters in the night, and there to wipe away tears.

Fathers had to work to keep up a home, but a Mother was on call 24 hours a day.

Her wages were based on the Love you gave; she performed her duties with little pay.

Children whine and complain, but Mothers have Patience to spare.

When her day is unsettled, she reaches in her Heart and finds Peace in God's Love that is there.

She spreads her Love like a blanket covering her Loved ones from want and harm.

When your day holds troubles, she gives you shelter in two Loving arms.

It's true that many Dear Mothers are in Heaven, but it will be easy to find.

Many signs of that Precious Mother's Love she left for you behind.

So take your Mother in your arms today, tell her what she means to you.

That Love she gives you has Blessed your Life, for God's Love is in it too.

The Smile Greeters remember their Mother's Love, too.

For they pass on that Love with God's Love to Bless your whole day through.

Our Love and a Smile ... Hattie D. & Nina

Two Loving Arms

Week 2—May 11, 2008

These few words of Praise, Dear Mama, are to say what you still mean to me.
You will ever Live in my Heart, my thoughts, and my memory.
'Mama, Mama!' I would cry out as a child, and in minutes, you would be there.
Ready to chase the dragon from my room back to his land of No Where.
'Mama, Mama!' I would cry out at play when I fell and skinned my knees.
I would run home to two Loving arms that gave comfort and made the pain cease.
How many times through my Life did that call go out for that very Loving care?
You were always ready with your Mother's Love. God gave you so much to share.
So many Mothers now walk with God, but they left such sweet memories behind.
Memories of their endless deeds of Love that will Live in their Loved One's mind.
The Smile Greeters remember their Dear Mothers, too.
For that Love they were given shows in the Smiles that they pass on to you.

Our Love and a Smile … Hattie D. & Nina

Appreciate the Senses

Week 3—May 18, 2008

The song came stealing into my sleep so clear on the morning breeze.

Twas the song of a small bird singing nearby somewhere in the trees.

As I listened to that joyful song, that was such music to the ear.

I humbly murmured a grateful Prayer, 'Thank You, Dear Lord, that I can hear.'

In the garden, flowers were blooming, their fragrance filled the air.

God's rainbow of colors that covered the earth grew in beauty everywhere.

A yellow daffodil smiling up at the sun was a true delight to me.

Again, Praise to God welled up within me, 'Thank God that I can see.'

If this were a World where all was silent, how strange it would be and bleak.

However, I can raise my voice in a song, 'Thank You, God, that I can speak.'

We take all these things so for granted, yet there is so very much more.

That we could bow our heads and say, 'Dear Lord, I am Thankful for..."

The Smile Greeters are very Thankful too …

For they pass on their Praise of God in the Smiles that they give to you.

> *Our Love and a Smile … Hattie D. & Nina*

A Memorial for Those We Love

Week 4—May 30, 2010

Today is an Honored Holiday that be stored in the Heart with memories that never cease.

Of Loved ones that gave their Love for us, that left such Happy memories.

But don't make it a day of mourning, for it holds many Loving memories too.

Remember our Service men and women who fought, and some are still in a war for me and you.

If you start your day with sadness, you are still Living in your yesterday.

There is too much Love in our Hearts to let it steal the Joy from the day.

Memorial Day is a day to remember with memories of Love, Joy, and Happiness.

Thank God for the Loved ones He gave you that are still with you to Love and to Bless.

I know that God remembers the day His Precious Loving Son died.

He gave His Life on the Cross for us, and by wicked men was scorned, even denied.

So Loved ones, you will remember and all the years of Love for you they left behind.

But also remember your Loving Friends and their Love God gives you to find.

The Smile Greeters all rejoice in this Holiday too.

For they remember the Love of the old members and look out for the Friendship of the new.

Our Love and a Smile ... Hattie D. & Nina

6-1-08

Memorial Day has come and gone do we now push that Honor for Loved ones aside?

No Indeed God planted that Love in our Hearts to Honor Loved ones who are Living or those who have died.

Memories are like a well read book They hold chapters of Love that reach back through the years.

Revealing precious moments shared by loved ones holding laughter and tears.

For some of us those moments are cherished for Loved ones now who are gone.

But for some that still have Loved ones God will keep that Love true and strong.

Memories are gifts of love that departed ones left behind for you.

But today you share love with Loved ones who one day will leave memories to.

The Waterview Church Smile Grieters no doubt hold memories of Love in their Heart.

Their Smiles show in the time of Loving memories they are very much a part.

    Our Love and a Smile
        Hallie D + Nina

Never Forget

Week 1—June 1, 2008

Memorial Day has come and gone; do we now push that Honor for Loved ones aside?

No indeed! God planted that Love in our Hearts to Honor Loved ones who are Living or those who have died.

Memories are like a well-read book; they hold chapters of Love that reach back through the years.

Revealing precious moments shared by Loved ones holding laughter and tears.

For some of us, those moments are cherished for Loved ones now who are gone.

But for some that still have Loved ones, God will keep that love true and strong.

Memories are gifts of Love that departed one left behind for you.

But today you share Love with Loved ones who one day will leave memories too.

The Smile Greeters no doubt hold memories of Love in their Heart.

Their Smiles show in the time of Loving memories, they are very much a part.

Our Love and a Smile ... Hattie D. & Nina

Saluting Our Fathers

Week 2—June 15, 2008

Mothers have rejoiced in their day of Honor, now Fathers deserve their Honor too.

So here's a Salute to all Fathers with our Love and Praise to all of you.

Thank you, Dear Fathers, for all of your years of hard labor that placed food on the table for us.

You would rise in the morning to maybe face a rough day with no complaint or fuss.

Thank you for helping us to be taught to Love and Respect our God's Holy Name.

That those principles should ever Live in our Hearts, and never ever change.

You followed God's instructions to guide your Loved ones in Faith, Belief, and Prayer.

You were never too busy if we needed help; your Love and Strength were there.

Now, some Beloved Fathers may be gone, we still Honor them with our Love.

They Live with our Heavenly Father, who we Honor in His Heaven up above.

The Smile Greeters Honor that Father with their Love, too.

For the Love that Shines within their Hearts lightens our Hearts too.

Our Love and a Smile ... Hattie D. & Nina

A "Faith" Lift

Week 3—June 17, 2007

Sometimes in Life we seem to need a Faith lift, it is true.

Well, here are a few suggestions on ways to lift your Faith, and lift your Spirit too ...

Go by your Church, there are Loving Smile Greeters faithfully standing by.

To give your weary Heart a cheerful lift, they certainly will try.

Just step into the Auditorium and you will have the great pleasure to hear,

God's Inspired Word from the Preacher that will make your Faith stand up and cheer.

Each time our Faith is tested by mountains we must climb,

They just won't seem that tall at all if we walk with Faith, one step at a time.

Our Love and a Smile ... Hattie D. & Nina

The ABC's of Greeting

Week 4—June 20, 2010

THINGS WE CAN BE from A to Z …

A—Accountable for whatever we do.
B—Benevolent, doing good for others.
C—Caring for those in need.
D—Devout in our Beliefs and Worship.
E—Encouraging to those who are down.
F—Faithful in our Worship.
G—Gentle in our ways and manners.
H—Helpful to all whenever we can.
I—Intelligent in reading the Bible, to stay smart.
J—Joyful in our Spirit.
K—Kind in all our actions and manners.
L - Loyal to our God and Friends.
M - Modest by not putting ourselves on a pedestal.
N—Nice to all those who aren't.
O—Orderly by keeping all things and thoughts in order.
P—Patient with all those who aren't.
Q—Quiet at times and listen to God.
R—Reverent ever to your Lord God.
S - Sincere in your Friendships.
T -Thankful ever for God's Grace.
U—Understanding to a Friend's troubles.
V - Vigilant ever in Life to avoid Sin.
W—Willing ever to sacrifice to God.
X—(E)XALT God to the Highest Degree.
Y—Yielding means giving in when someone disagrees.
Z—Zealous when you are doing God's Work.
The Smile Greeters display these qualities to all who are passing by.
They know it is the true Love of God, for Rainbows fill the sky.

Our Love and a Smile … Hattie D. & Nina

7-8-07 M

Sometime ago I heard someone say it was God crying each time we had a rain.
A sign of His sadness for all of our Sins the tears from a Heart of pain.
So as I sat today watching the rain falling down I ask myself "Was it I?"
That because of some sin on my part gave Him anguish and made Him cry.
Sometimes we put the blame on others for the wrong things we think they may do.
When we should stop and look into our own Lives and examine our own actions to.
Whether rain or shine the Waterview Church Smile Greeters set an example at the door
And they use Gods Love as an umbrella that shields us from the storms of Life and more.
We are each responsible how we Live our Lives so we never have to ask "Was it I?"
That turned away from His Blessed teachings and in our sinning made Him cry.
 Our Love and a Smile ☺
 Hattie D + Nina

God's Tears

Week 1—July 8, 2007

Sometime ago, I heard someone say it was God crying each time we had a rain.

A sign of His sadness for all of our Sins, the tears from a Heart of pain.

So as I sat today watching the rain falling down, I asked myself, 'Was it I?'

That because of some sin on my part gave Him anguish and made Him cry?

Sometimes we put the blame on others for the wrong things we think they may do.

When we should stop and look into our owns Lives and examine our own actions too.

Whether rain or shine, the Smile Greeters set an example at the door.

And they use God's Love as an umbrella that shields us from the storms of Life and more.

We are each responsible how we Live our Lives, so we never have to ask, 'Was it I?'

That turned away from His Blessed teachings, and in our sinning made Him cry.

Our Love and a Smile … Hattie D. & Nina

A Goodnight Prayer

Week 2—July 19, 2009

When you retire for the night and for some reason you can't get to sleep,
Stop and think how much a Prayer can do instead of counting sheep.
Perhaps your Prayer to God can help a Loved one who is in a time of despair.
For that, Prayer of Love and concern will reach God, and He, with His Love, will be there.
In a faraway part of the World, stressed Soldiers in a War truly need Prayers too.
God knows of their danger and fear, but He patiently waits to hear from you.
For He knows if there is Faith and Love in your Heart, World Peace will be a concern.
So, to get those Prayers answered, God is the only true way to turn.
Take a moment to Pray for the hungry and the homeless and what they are going through.
Tell God how Blessed you feel those things aren't happening to you.
Now your eyes are getting sleepy, and you feel content knowing the good a Prayer can do.
Peace and Rest will be yours through the night, for God cares for your welfare, too.
The Smile Greeters are ready with their Prayers, too.
For they know what the Power of God's Love and Faith can do.

Our Love and a Smile ... Hattie D. & Nina

If God Were Too Busy

Week 3—July 26, 2008

Sometimes we get caught up in this busy World and sadly we forget to Pray.

What would we do if God did the same, and forgot the world for a day?

There would be no Sun to light up the day after a morning rain.

There would be no God to comfort us through our many trials and pain.

No Heavenly Father to help with our burdens when we traveled over a rough road.

No strength of Loving arms to lift and help us to carry our heavy load.

There would be no Heavenly Father to answer if repentant sinners should call.

No caring God to lift us up if straying Christians should stumble and fall.

Yes, this World would be a forsaken place if God really forgot it for a day.

So read His Holy Word, strive every day to Live it, and never ever forget to Pray.

Our Smile Greeters stand each Sunday with a Smile of Cheer.

That says to everyone, God will never be absent ... open the door, come on in, your Loving God is here.

Our Love and a Smile ... Hattie D. & Nina

Nursing Home

Week 4—July 26, 2009

Flowers in bloom are a beautiful sight, but with time they wither away.
Still, we know in Spring they will bloom again with beauty another day.
So it is with our Nursing Home aged who once Lived a Life young and gay.
Now their faces show lines from years of care, their hair in shades of gray.
Their hands, once busy with endless tasks, are stiff and idle now, it's true.
But once they were gentle and so filled with Love, with deeds of Love done for you.
It may seem in the affairs of Life you are forgotten and don't have a place.
But you have left your mark of Love on <u>all</u> … that time will never erase.
Your Loved ones are Blessed with that Love you gave, and your sacrifices too.
For through their many trials in Life, God and you brought them safely through.
The Smile Greeters also send their Love your way today.
For perhaps they have a Loved one in a Home that Blessed them along Life's way.

Our Love and a Smile … Hattie D. & Nina

8-2-09

When I was a child and a Doctor was needed night or day he would come and hold your hand.

He would sometimes say "I don't know what causes your illness but I shall try to understand."

Now today its entirely different each Doctor treats a different illness all its own.

Some are diseases that through the years without a cure have definetly grown.

Some Doctors dont have the Heart to treat you their attitudes are "Take a pill and Pay your bill".

But dont lose Heart we have a Loving Physician who with Faith and Prayer to cure you He certainly will.

His medicines are Love, Hope and Comfort His Healing Love is free there is no pay.

So let others know of that Healing Love He is available twenty four hours a day.

The Waterview Church Smile Greeters

A Doctor's Hands

Week 1—August 2, 2009

When I was a child and a Doctor was needed, night or day, he would come and hold your hand.

He would sometimes say, 'I don't know what causes your illness, but I shall try to understand.'

Now, today it's entirely different; each Doctor treats a different illness all its own.

Some are diseases that, through the years, without a cure, have definitely grown.

Some Doctors don't have the Heart to treat you; their attitudes are 'Take a pill and pay your bill.'

But don't lose Heart. We have a Loving Physician who, with Faith and Prayer, will certainly cure you.

His medicines are Love, Hope, and Comfort ... His Healing Love is free; there is no pay.

So let others know of that Healing Love, He is available twenty-four hours a day.

The Smile Greeters stand ready at the door to show you the way.

With our Care in the Loving hands of God, our troubles are not here to stay.

Our Love and a Smile ... Hattie D. & Nina

God's Gifts

Week 2—August 16, 2009

We mortals tend to take in stride each gift our Lord bestows.
Our health and wealth we wear with Pride and make certain that it shows.
We Live each day without a thought of giving Thanks to God.
We walk amid the beauty given along each path we trod.
We listen to a small bird's song, he is so eager to sing.
And never give a sign we heard the sound of anything.
I sometimes feel that God on high must give up in despair.
But all He seems to do is sigh and give more Loving care.
The Smile Greeters are on the job to please their God, too.
And are Happy to pass on the Love God gives so freely to me and you.

Our Love and a Smile ... Hattie D. & Nina

A Hurried Prayer

Week 3—August 19, 2007

I knelt to Pray, but not for long, I had too much to do.
I must hurry off and get to work, for bills soon would be due.
And so, I said a hurried Prayer and jumped up off my knees.
My Christian duty now was done; my Soul could rest at ease.
All through the day, I had no time to speak a word of cheer.
No time to speak of Christ to Friends, they would laugh at me I feared.
No time, no time, too much to do, that was my constant cry.
No time to give to those in need … At last, it was my time to die.
And when before the Lord I came, I stood with downcast eyes.
Within His hands, He held a Book, it was the Book of Life.
God looked into His Book and said, 'Your Name I cannot find.
I once was going to write it down, but I never found the time.'
So, my advice, my Friend, be like the Smile Greeters … obey the Lord for
    when He stops to look,
He will find your Name in no time at all … written down in His Precious
    Book.

Our Love and a Smile … Hattie D. & Nina

Advice to the Youth

Week 4—August 22, 2010

I once heard a young teen make the remark, 'Just wait till I reach twenty-one.
I will be my own Boss and there will be no end of activities or fun.'
But please, kids, don't wish to grow up too soon; the years go by mighty fast.
Enjoy your young life while you're young, try to make that happy time last.
Remember your joyous days as a kid, when you were young and carefree.
For the years fly by and you age, and youth will soon be just a memory.
Some good advice, young people, learn to know God, He will tell you what to do.
He is so wise about all the problems you will face, and He will guide you safely through.
Remember, He was once a teenager too, and He will never guide you wrong.
If you stumble and fall, He will lift you up and set you right where you belong.
So, enjoy and have fun in your childhood years, and if a problem happens to you,
Just ask your guide who is ever by your side, 'Jesus, what would you do?'
The Smile Greeters claim Him as their Daily Guide.
And with a Loving Smile upon their face proves God is by their side.

Our Love and a Smile ... Hattie D. & Nina

Use Your Talent

Week 5—August 30, 2009

You tell me you think that I have a Talent in writing the Poetry that I do.

Well, Dear ones, Talent is a God given gift, so you each have a Talent too.

The Ministers have an Inspiring Talent in the way God's Word is brought to you.

The Love of God comes through in their Sermons that ring in our Hearts so true.

The Song Leader's voice is a Talent, using his voice to Praise our Savior in song.

It winds its way to Heaven, and the Heavenly Choir joyfully sings along.

Now, each member of the Church has a Special Talent too, that was given to each Loving one.

It's the Talent of Love and Caring that shows in your Loving deeds being done.

Those are the true qualities of Talent that was put into each Heart by our God above.

Simple, worthwhile gifts of God that are Blessed by His everlasting Love.

The Smile Greeters have their share of Talent, too.

For they pass on God's Love that will make your Faith bright and uplifting to you.

Our Love and a Smile ... Hattie D. & Nina

9-7-08

It is enough that I have seen the Sun slip behind the hills like a golden ball.

To rise in splendor on a brand new day I need no other proof if this were all.

It is enough for me that I have watched the Moon, the Stars, the Seasons as they come and go.

The Day for work the Night for restful sleep who but a Loving God could plan things so.

This is enough the Miracle of birth the growing seeds that pushed up through the sod.

The inner voice that stills all reasons of doubt I need no other proof there is a God.

The Waterview Church Smile Greeters show their belief in God to they show His Love in their beautiful Smile.

That sign of Gods Love puts a spark in the day and never goes out of style.

Our Love and a Smile
Hattie D & Nina

It is Enough . . .

Week 1—September 7, 2008

It is enough that I have seen the Sun slip behind the hills like a golden ball.

To rise in splendor on a brand-new day, I need no other proof if this were all.

It is enough for me that I have watched the Moon, the Stars, the Seasons as the come and go.

The Day for work, the Night for restful sleep, who but a Loving God could plan things so?

This is enough, the Miracle of birth, the growing seeds that push up through the sod.

The inner voice that stills all reasons of doubt, I need no other proof there is a God.

The Smile Greeters show their belief in God, too; they show His Love in their beautiful Smile.

That sign of God's Love puts a spark in the day, and never goes out of style.

Our Love and a Smile . . . Hattie D. & Nina

Choosing Your Words

Week 2—September 13, 2009

God gives us the choice to say the right Words; did you use the right ones today?
Or did you take the joy from someone's hour and turn their blue skies to gray?
A few bitter Words said in anger can bring a sad feeling to the Lord.
For He wants us to Live with the Love He gave us in our deeds, actions, and Words.
For unpleasant Words and bitter Words, only fools can think to say.
But the hurt they leave behind them, many years can't wipe away.
A little bit of thoughtlessness can spoil a number of otherwise Happy years.
And leave behind memories of unkind thoughts and deeds in remembered tears.
So, erase any unkind thoughts that are whirling around in your head.
And only remember the Sacred Words that our Loving Savior ever said.
The Smile Greeters only have God's Loving Words to say . . .
To each one that enters, they give a Smile and say, 'God's Love be yours today.'

Our Love and a Smile . . . Hattie D. & Nina

Who is Important?

Week 3—September 14, 2008

Sometimes when you're feeling important, sometime when self-importance is in bloom.
Sometime when you take it for granted, You're the best qualified in the room.
Sometime when you feel that you're going would leave an unfillable hole.
Just follow this simple instruction and see how it humbles your Soul.
Take a bucket and fill it with water, put your hand in it up to the wrist.
Pull it out and the hole that remains is a measure of how you'll be missed.
You may splash all you want when you enter, you can stir up the water galore.
But stop and you'll find in a moment that it looks just like it did before.
The moral in this written example is ... do the very best that you can.
Be proud of yourself and remember, God made no indispensable man.

Our Love and a Smile ... Hattie D. & Nina

A Seed of Wisdom

Week 4—September 23, 2007

What is a Word but a group of letters that can be spoken or written down.

A Word can hold a Holy feeling of Reverence or hold the humor of a Clown.

Each Word is like a seed of Wisdom just waiting to be sown.

For Words hold many meanings, each one holds a message all its own.

There's a Happy feeling in the Word 'Hello,' sometimes sadness in 'Goodbye.'

A tender Word conveys a message of Love; a harsh Word can make you cry.

The Smile Greeters have a secret Word heartily approved by God ... the Word is SMILE.

It fits on the face of everyone and never ever goes out of style.

Sometimes it's important in a contest to choose the right Word to win.

But it just took one Inspired Word of God to Create a World, and our Lives to begin.

Our Love and a Smile ... Hattie D. & Nina

10-11-09

When you receive a gift from a Loved
one or a Friend.
   You do the proper Thing a Thank You
note you send.
   When you need some assistance for
a task that you must do.
   And someone lends a hand you
gladly say "Thank You".
   If ever you're rejected and there is
sadness you must bear.
   To those who ease your burdens
just say Thank You for their Care.
   And when your Trials are over
and Faithfully you Pray.
   Don't ask for many other Things
just say "Thank You for this day".
   Each Blessing is a gift That comes
from up above.
   God knows exactly what you need
just say "Thank You Lord with Love".
   When we trust Him with our needs
our troubles soon will fade away.
   When we rest in the Glory of another

What to Do with a Gift

Week 1—October 11, 2009

When you receive a gift from a Loved one or a Friend,
You do the proper thing, a 'Thank You' note you send.
When you need some assistance for a task that you must do,
And someone lends a hand, you gladly say, 'Thank You.'
If ever you're rejected and there is sadness you must bear,
To those who ease your burdens, just say, Thank You for your Care.
And when your trials are over and Faithfully you Pray,
Don't ask for many other things, just say 'Thank You for this day.'
Each Blessing is a gift that comes from up above.
God knows exactly what you need ... just say 'Thank You, Lord' with Love.
When we trust Him with our needs, our troubles soon will fade away.
When we rest in the Glory of another Blessed day.
The Smile Greeters are eager to show their gratitude, too.
For they know that God is pleased for Caring things they do.

Our Love and a Smile ... Hattie D. & Nina

Loving Words

Week 2—October 12, 2008

There are so many Loving words that are dancing around in your head.

For Heaven's sake, give them to someone now, don't let them vanish instead.

There are so many people deserving of that Love for deeds they have done for you.

Give them some of those Loving words, tell them their reward is due.

Next, tell the Minister what a wonderful sermon he gives to your listening ear.

Tell the Song Leader you are Happy with the songs of God's Love he chooses for you to hear.

How about your Loving Friends that you worship with each week?

Did you give them some of those Loving words, they would Love to hear you speak?

The Smile Greeters in their Hearts have Loving words too.

They follow God's commands and give those Loving words as gifts, as we all should do.

Our Love and a Smile ... Hattie D. & Nina

Our Chartered Life

Week 3—October 14, 2007

So many times, I have heard someone say, 'If I could live my life over again…'
If this were possible, could they, in their New Life, eliminate all hardships and pain?
God chartered our Lives with His Love and Wisdom, so let's Live it as He has planned.
For along the way, if the journey gets rough, He is there with Love and a helping hand.
No one's Life will ever be trouble free, there will be burdens, sorrow, and stress.
But that Loving God is standing by ready to Love, Comfort, and Bless.
So, don't wish to go back, you will find nothing there that you don't have with you today.
Whatever you need, whatever you lack, God will Bless you in His way.
The Smile Greeters are (standing) faithfully by,
Ready to give so free from their Heart, God's Love and a Smile to you and I.

Our Love and a Smile … Hattie D. & Nina

Preparing for Sunday Morning

Week 4—October 21, 2007

Each Sunday morning, in getting ready for Church, I prepare for a journey of Love.

I have a wonderful Guide that goes with me, the Loving Father up above.

The first step is the Church, and the Loyal Smile Greeters waiting there.

Ready to give their Smiles and Love, God said we all must share.

The next stop is our Bible Study Class taught by a Special God Loving man.

Who instills in our Hearts how to Live our Life for God and how to follow His plan.

Now I face the last step of the journey, to hear a Sermon about God so vital and true.

From a dedicated Believing Preacher who teaches Love and God's grace to you.

Now the Sermons are over, and I prepare to go home, do I leave that Love behind?

No, indeed! I bring that Love with me where it shall ever be there to find.

Our Love and a Smile ... Hattie D. & Nina

A Sleepless Night

Week 5—October 25, 2009

Some night, when you are lying in bed, and sleep won't come to you.
Just listen to the sounds of the night that seem to come stealing through.
It's surprising what sounds you can hear for the night is never still.
It's much more entertaining and much better than a sleeping pill.
For a minute or two, there is silence, then a dog barks in the neighborhood.
Somewhere, another dog takes up the cry as if the barking he understood.
Suddenly, a motorcycle shatters the night with a rumble that goes on and on.
It roars down the street, turns a distant corner … the noise fades and is gone.
An ambulance siren wails in the night as it races to someone in pain.
Racing against traffic and time, Praying their journey isn't in vain.
The sounds of the night finally fade away, and it soon will be time to arise.
So, what to do? You snuggle down in bed and close those now sleepy eyes.
The Smile Greeters stand ready to greet the early morn.
Ready to show their Love of God in Happy Smiles that are worn.

Our Love and a Smile … Hattie D. & Nina

11-2-08

Whatever food you take on your plate
if too much and its thrown away.
Have a thought for all that are hungry
that would Love that food Today.
We take our abundance of things for granted
that in plenty will always be there.
But what we do have is Gods gift to us
and to others we must share.
We live in a land of plenty for America
has been Blessed by God we truly know.
He has Blessed our soil with a richness
that makes our produce flourish and grow.
There are homeless people living on the
street facing hopelessness and asking the
question "Why"?
While we in self contentment and well
being say "There but for the Grace of God
go I".
Dont ever take what you have for
granted and for others have not a care.
Take Gods Word from the Bible and to
God and to those in need give of your
abundance and share
The Waterview Church Smile Greeters
give a gift of Gods Love to you.

In Our Abundance

Week 1—November 2, 2008

Whatever food you take on your plate, if too much and it's thrown away,
Have a thought for all that are hungry that would Love that food today.
We take our abundance of things for granted, that in plenty will always be there.
But what we do have is God's gift to us and to others, we must share.
We live in a land of plenty, for America has been Blessed by God, we truly know.
He has Blessed our soil with a richness that makes our produce flourish and grow.
There are homeless people living on the street, facing hopelessness and the question, 'Why?'
While we, in self-contentment and well-being, say, 'There but for the Grace of God, go I.'
Don't ever take what you have for granted, and for others have not a care.
Take God's Word from the Bible, and to God and to those in need give of your abundance and share.
The Smile Greeters give a gift of God's Love to you.
For it's in that Smile to you; they give God of their abundance too.

Our Love and a Smile ... Hattie D. & Nina

I Place My Hand in Yours

Week 2—November 4, 2007

Each morning when I wake and say, 'God, I place my hand in Yours today.
With Faith and Trust that by my side You will walk with me and my steps,
*   You will guide.'*
God leads me with the tenderest care
When my Path is dark, and I despair.
No need for me to question or try to understand,
If I just keep my Faith and hold fast to His hand.
His Welfare is ever there for me, and by His generous bounty, I am fed.
He grants me Peace, and by His great Love, I am warmed and comforted.
When the day has ended, and I quietly seek my rest,
I look back at the wonder He has given me and I know I have been Blessed.
I say a Prayer and Thank my God for the great day it has been.
And in the morning, I start the day by placing my hand in His again.

Our Love and a Smile … Hattie D. & Nina

Today's Hero

Week 3—November 9, 2008

This is the time of year when all Veterans are Honored for service performed in the War.

Wishing all of them the Love of God and Blessings He has in store.

America is full of Heroes; you don't have far to search.

For we have many who fit that Title right in the Lord's church.

Just what makes a Hero, God made all men equal, it's true.

It's a man who answers a country's call for help but obeys God's Commands too.

He carried a burden in his Heart, for it was God's Commandment, 'Thou Shalt Not Kill.'

But it was the Army Commander who said, 'At any cost, we must conquer that hill.'

God created all men equal to Live his Life in his individual way.

And for those who chose to follow God's will, makes him a Hero every day.

Your share of Glory is in the part you played to make this World a better place.

By being an example to your fellow man and make them desire God's Love and Redeeming Grace.

The Smile Greeters are sort of Heroes to me and you.

Their Smiles are an invitation to enlist in God's Army, too.

Our Love and a Smile ... Hattie D. & Nina

Beautiful Blessings

Week 4—November 23, 2008

This is the time of year when Praise our God for deeds we're so Thankful for.

We have Lived with a Lifetime of Blessings that He ever has in Store.

We bow our heads to You, Dear Lord, in Thanks for all You have done.

You gave something so Precious to the World, Your very own Dearly Beloved Son.

November is a Thankful time, and every Heart is truly Blessed.

For at our table of Loved ones and wonderful food, Jesus is our Special Guest.

You gave us gifts of Beautiful Friends who shared their Love along the way.

And on Sunday morning a Man of God to preach God's Love and to sing and Pray.

May we never take for granted those many Loving Blessings we receive.

But prove our Love by the way we Live with Your Precious Word in our Hearts that believe.

The Smile Greeters show they are very Thankful too.

By the way they give God's Love in their Smiles ... and pass them on as gifts to you.

Our Love and a Smile ... Hattie D. & Nina

An Extra Poem for Veterans

November 8, 2009

You marched away some years ago, your heads held high and proud.

Ready to carry out your service to your country you had Faithfully vowed.

So, on Veterans Day, we pause to give a Heart full of Praise to you.

You all had a Leader you believed in; it was God who would see you safely through.

We Salute you, men who fought so long ago and those that are fighting today.

For we know your duties were done with a Faithful Heart, performed in God's Holy Way.

It was Hate that was the cause of your marching away, but God's Love brought you home again.

His Love was the shield for your safety, so your activities weren't all in vain.

There were many brave men that didn't march away, but they fought an enemy too.

Their Love and Vigilance to Loved ones left behind help a Prayer that God would see them through.

May each of you on the Road of Life find a smooth and trouble-free Road.

And may your Hearts be lifted on wings of Love for Blessings God has sowed.

Our Love and a Smile ... Hattie D. & Nina

12-6-09

There is a gift that is sure to please more precious than pure gold.

A gift that is meant for everyone from the young to the very old.

It is a very common gift that is impossible to hide.

And oh so very popular its easily found World wide.

It is a very fragile gift that should be nourished with great care.

And although it is quite common it can also be quite rare.

Every one at times has had it people enjoy it every day.

But it seems to have more value. when it is freely given away.

Even though this gift is priceless its no good to us unless.

We share this gift with others this great gift known as Happiness.

The Waterview Church Smile Greeters share their Love to all who come their way.

A Rare Gift

Week 1—December 6, 2009

There is a gift that is sure to please, more precious than pure gold.
A gift that is meant for everyone, from the young to the very old.
It is a very common gift that is impossible to hide.
And oh, so very popular, it's easily found Worldwide.
It is a very fragile gift that should be nourished with great care.
And although it is quite common, it can also be quite rare.
Everyone, at times, has had it; people enjoy it every day.
But it seems to have more value when it is freely given away.
Even though this gift is priceless, it's no good to us unless ...
We share this gift with others, this great gift known as Happiness.
The Smile Greeters share their Love to all who come their way.
And the Happiness they have comes from God, who says, 'Sow it to all today.'

Our Love and a Smile ... Hattie D. & Nina

My Christmas List

Week 2—December 9, 2007

I had my Christmas list made out; it seemed the longest one in town.
But in checking it over, I realized I would have to cut that long list down.
I truly had to do it over; there surely was no doubt.
For the fact that really shook me up was I had left our Dearest Lord out.
So, I scanned my Christmas list again and said to myself, 'It can't be true.'
That I would leave out the very Dear One who gave His Life for you.
It was our Jesus whom I had neglected to add on to my list.
The Holy One that should Live our Hearts and never, ever be missed.
It didn't take me long at all to change my Christmas list about.
For in His Love and Care for us, He never ever leaves us out.
The Smile Greeters pass out a Smile that anyone passing by can't miss.
For that Smile shows their Love for Jesus, and that He is Number One on their list.

Our Love and a Smile ... Hattie D. & Nina

The Greatest Gift

Week 3—December 13, 2009

The greatest gift at Christmas time is one we all can give.
God's Love from the Heart that makes Life a joy to Live.
A kind thought or a helping hand to show someone we care.
To let them know how much it means to us just to have them there.
The greatest gift at Christmas time costs not a cent to buy.
It's being a Loving neighbor as the years go passing by.
It's offering a helping hand when someone needs a lift.
And so, I Pray at this Christmas time that this may be your gift.
Jesus came so we could be forgiven for our sins.
He is searching for receptive Hearts that will invite Him in.
If we accept His offer and in Him alone believe.
Eternal Life is the greatest gift we ever shall receive.
The Smile Greeters give a Smile right from their Heart.
That Smile shows in God's Love ... they are very much a part.

Our Love and a Smile ... Hattie D. & Nina

What I Wish For

Week 4—December 14, 2008

Do you know what I wish for you this Christmas? Nothing you'll find in a store.
But gifts that will Live in your Heart when the Holly is gone from your door.
I wish you the gift of true Friendship, as warm as Holiday Cheer.
The kind that will bring your Heart Joy each day of the coming year.
I wish you the gift of good health, good fortune in all that you do.
I wish you a time for Prayer each day, your Spirit to renew.
I also wish for you this Christmas a Special gift that is set apart.
I wish you the gift of the Christ Child, Living each day in your Heart.
May we accept the gift of Love that Christmas time imparts.
And may God's Angels sing in Heaven, and also in our Hearts.
The Smile Greeters wish a Merry Christmas to you.
And say, 'God's Blessing to you and yours every day all year through.'

Our Love and a Smile ... Hattie D. & Nina

Christmas Thieves

Week 5—December 16, 2007

I have a concern of thieves in the World and the Holy things they are trying to steal.

And I Pray when you hear just what they are that concern you, too, will feel.

First, they are trying to hide our Ten Holy Commandments; they say they are displeasing to the eye.

Well, those Laws are very Sacred to us, for God teaches us how to Live, you and I.

Next, they are trying to take Christ out of Christmas by wanting us to change it to 'Have a Happy Holiday.'

But they won't stop my 'Merry Christmas,' Jesus Christ is in my Heart, and there He will stay.

Now it's our moment of Silent Prayer that concerns them; they say God doesn't hear a Word.

Well, maybe they can't hear them, but God can ... and each thought from the Heart is heard.

Now you ask, 'Who are 'They' that's trying so hard to steal God's Holy Words away?'

It's Satan's army of nonbelievers that question our Faith every day.

The Smile Greeters stand up for God with their Love and Smile.

Satan will never weaken their Faith for they walk with Jesus every wonderful mile.

Our Love and a Smile ... Hattie D. & Nina

A Personal, and Final, Thank You

(from Hattie to Mike)

"I know that you had a loving mother and dad, for they instilled a love in you.
For that love shines out, dearest friend, in all you say and do.
You take two little old ladies and make them feel like Queens for a day.
You have an extra sparkle about you that, for many, makes a brighter way.
You are a very special kind of fellow, Mike. I know there are many who have told you so.
And I want to tell you the joy your friendship means to me, the older that I grow.
When my journey through life is over and my travels come to an end,
I shall face my Dear Lord and say, 'I thank you and praise you for the gift that blessed my life, the gift of a Wonderful Friend."

All my Love … Hattie D.

From Hattie's Hand

A Dismal World without a Smile

1-25-09

Wouldn't this be a dismal World if no one ever Smiled at you.
It would be like a dark cloud between Heaven and Earth where Gods Love couldn't shine Through.
But God said No that can never be so He gave everyone a Beautiful Smile.
A frown on the face is out of date a Loving Smile is more in style.
So He gave the Waterview Church Smile Greeters a very important place.
At the Door of the Church Gods Love shining on their face.
So show you're in style by that Loving Smile that God Lives in your Heart.
For the World needs that Love from God to know in that Love they are a part.
Don't ever get too busy you don't have time to talk to God for awhile.
And you will find you are facing all of Lifes problems with a Smile.
Our Love and a Smile.
Nattie D & Nina

Wrapped in Love

2-18-07

A Smile is a kindness wrapped in Love did you give one of yours today.
That Smile will light up a cloudy day and chase dark clouds away.
If we all would take the time to give a Smile to someone in place of a frown.
We could all help the World be a better place with Gods approval Smiling down.
Today there may be tears in your Heart But theres also a Smile living there
For the Waterview Church Smile Greeters gave one of Gods Loving Smiles to share.
So if you give someone the gift of your Smile feel content you did your part
To bring a ray of Sunshine Love that will grow in someones Heart.
Our Love and a Smile
Hattie D + Nina

Hold on Tight

3-27-11

The Sun is always shining although at times it cant be found.
Clouds of depression seem to hide it where suffering and misery abound.
Some days are dark and dreary but our Faith can pull us through.
If only we will be patient the sky will again be blue.
If we but trust and hold on Tight and never give in to despair.
Soon we will see a ray of light to let us know its there.
Yes we shall see the Sun shine again we shall see its radiant glow.
The Clouds will always fade away it is Gods Plan you know.
I believe that our God hears us always any time, anywhere.
When the load of Lifes troubles are lifted to prove He answers Prayer.
We must be sure to hold out a hand give a word of Love and a Smile.
To help the Friend beside you walk across each weary mile.
The Waterview Church Smile Greeters

A Key to God's Storehouse

4-13-08

The day may be a cloudy one and maybe hold a chance for showers.
But the Waterview Church of Smile Greeters are there with their Smiles like beautiful flowers.
Now a Smile on your face shows that that God Lives within and His Love is shining through.
So just try it once give someone a Smile and see what they will do.
Did you give someone a Smile today if you did you will get one back.
For Smiles are a key to Gods Store House of Love and that Love you will never lack.
Never leave kind words unspoken greet each one you meet with a Smile.
For that sign of Gods Love lightens many Hearts and makes one feel worth while.
God gives us that Loving Smile on our face but He tells us to give it away.
So look for someone who needs a lift and give them Gods gift today.
   Our Love and a Smile.
    Nattie D + Nina

A Hurried Prayer

8-19-07

I knelt to Pray but not for long
I had too much to do.
I must hurry off and get to work for
bills soon would be due.
And so I said a hurried Prayer and
jumped up off my knees.
My Christian duty now was done
my Soul could rest at ease.
All through the day I had no time
to speak a word of cheer.
No time to speak of Christ to Friends
they would laugh at me I feared.
No time, no time too much to do
That was my constant cry.
No time to give to those in need
at last it was my time to die.
And when before the Lord I came
I stood with downcast eyes.
Within His hands He held a Book
it was the Book of Life.
God looked into His Book and said
your Name I cannot find.
I once was going to write it down
but I never found the time.
So my advice my Friend be like
the Waterview Church Smile Greeters,
obey the Lord for when He stops to look.
He will find your Name in no time
at all written down in His Precious Book
Our Love and a Smile ☺
Hattie D + Nina

A Seed of Wisdom

9-23-07

What is a Word but a group of letters that can be spoken or written down.

A Word can hold a Holy feeling of Reverence or hold the humor of a Clown.

Each Word is like a seed of Wisdom just waiting to be sown.

For Words hold many meanings each one holds a message all its own.

Theres a Happy feeling in the Word Hello sometimes Sadness in Goodbye.

A tender Word conveys a message of Love a harsh Word can make you cry.

The Waterview Church Smile Greeters have a secret Word heartily approved by God the Word is SMILE

It fits on the face of everyone and never ever goes out of style.

Sometimes its important in a contest to choose the right Word to win

But it just took one Inspired Word God to Create a World and our Lives to begin.   Our Love and a Smile
Hattie D + Nina

Loving Words

10-12-08

There are so many Loving words that are dancing around in Your head

For Heaven sake give them to someone now dont let them vanish instead.

There are so many people deserving of that Love for deeds They have done for you.

Give Them some of those Loving words tell them their reward is due.

Next tell the Minister Robert Oglesby what a wonderful sermon he gives to your listening ear.

Tell the Song Leader Myron you are Happy with the songs of Gods Love he chooses for you to hear.

How about your Loving Friends that you worship with each week.

Did you give them some of those Loving words they would Love to hear you speak.

The Waterview Church Smile Greeters in their Hearts have Loving words to.

They follow Gods commands and give those Loving words as gifts as we all should do.

Our Love and a Smile

HATTIE & NINA

Christmas Thieves

12-16-07

I have a concern of Thieves in the World and the Holy things they are trying to steal.

And I Pray when you hear just what they are that concern you to will feel.

First they are trying to hide our Ten Holy Commandments they say they are displeasing to the eye.

Well these Laws are very Sacred to us for God teaches us how to Live you and I.

Next they are trying to take Christ out of Christmas by wanting us to change it to Have a Happy Holiday

But they won't stop my Merry Christmas Jesus Christ is in my Heart and there He will stay.

Now its our moment of Silent Prayer that concerns them they say God doesn't hear a Word.

Well maybe they can't hear them but God can and each thought from the Heart is heard.

Now you ask who are They thats trying so hard to steal Gods Holy Words away.

Its Satans army of non believers that question our Faith every day.

The Waterview Church Smile Greeters stand up for God with their Love and Smile.

Satan will never weaken their Faith for they walk with Jesus every wonderful mile

Our Love and a Smile
Hattie B + Nina

Whatever Food You Take

11-2-08

Whatever food you take on your plate if too much and its thrown away.
Have a thought for all that are hungry that would Love that food today.
We take our abundance of things for granted that in plenty will always be there.
But what we do have is Gods gift to us and to others we must share.
We live in a land of plenty for America has been Blessed by God we truly know.
He has Blessed our soil with a richness that makes our produce flourish and grow.
There are homeless people living on the street facing hopelessness and asking the question "Why"?
While we in self contentment and well being say "There but for the Grace of God go I".
Dont ever take what you have for granted and for others have not a care.
Take Gods Word from the Bible and to God and to those in need give of your abundance and share.
The Waterview Church Smile Greeters give a gift of Gods Love to you.

For its in that Smile to you,
they give God of their abundance to
Our Love and a Smile
Hattie D + Nina

M

Flowers in Bloom

7-26-09

Flowers in bloom are a beautiful sight but with time they wither away.

Still we know in Spring they will bloom again with beauty another day.

So it is with our Nursing Home aged who once Lived a Life young and gay.

Now their faces show lines from years of care their hair in shades of gray.

Their hands once busy with endless tasks are stiff and idle now its true.

But once they were gentle and so filled with Love with deeds of Love done for you.

It may seem in the affairs of Life you are forgotten and dont have a place.

But You have left your mark of Love on all that time will never erase.

Your Loved ones are Blessed with that Love you gave and your sacrifices to

For through their many trials in Life God and you brought them safely through.

The Waterview Church Smile Greeters also send their Love your way today.

For perhaps they have a Loved one in a Home that Blessed them along Lifes way

Our Love and a Smile ツ
Hattie D + Nina

Special Talents Given

8-30-04

You tell me you think that I have a Talent in writing the Poetry that I do.

Well Dear ones Talent is a God given gift so you each have a Talent to.

The Ministers have an Inspiring Talent in the way Gods Word is brought to you.

The Love of God comes through in their Sermons that ring in our Hearts so true.

The Song Leaders voice is a Talent using his voice to Praise our Saviour in song.

It wends its way to Heaven and the Heavenly Choir joyfully sing along.

Now each member of the Church has a Special Talent to that was given to each Loving one.

Its the Talent of Love and Caring that shows in your Loving deeds being done

Those are the true qualities of Talent that was put into each Heart by our God above.

Simple worth while gifts of Gods that are Blessed by His everlasting Love.

The Waterview Church Smile Greeters have their share of Talent to.

For they pass on Gods Love that
will make your Faith bright
and uplifting to you
Our Love and a Smile ☺
   Hattie D + Nina

☺

M

The Greatest Gift

12-13-09

The greatest gift at Christmas time is one we all can give.

Gods Love from the Heart that makes Life a joy to Live.

A kind thought or a helping hand to show someone we care.

To let them know how much it means to us just to have them there

The greatest gift at Christmas time costs not a cent to buy.

Its being a Loving neighbor as the years go passing by.

Its offering a helping hand when Someone needs a lift.

And so I Pray at this Christmas time that this may be your gift

Jesus came so we could be forgivin for our sins.

He is searching for receptive Hearts that will invite Him in.

If we accept His offer and in Him alone believe

Eternal Life is the greatest gift

we ever shall receive
The Waterview Church Smile Greeters give a Smile right from their Heart. That Smile shows in Gods Love they are very much a part.
   Our Love and a Smile ☺
   Nattie D + Nina

Four Types of Vegetables

1-17-10

There are numerous vegetables in the World but I've narrowed it down to four.

They are only ordinary Tators but each has their own personality and more.

First we have the Agitators who try to stir up trouble wherever they go.

They have no regard for Rules or Laws but their know it all manner they Love to show.

Next we have the Hesitators who always question what they should do.

Their Church truly needs their aid but they could use a new car to.

Now we have the commentators who always have plenty to say.

He tries to steer the conversation to where he comes out top man of the day.

Last but not least is the old Sweet tator he Lives every day to help his Friends.

He strives to follow Gods Plan of Love and his quest never ends.
  We are greeted By the Waterview Smile Greeters every Sunday passing on Gods Love So true.
  As we enter in lets think and ponder which Tator applies to you?
    Our Love and a Smile
      Hattie D + Nina

Do We Need the Snow?

2-28-10

Down it came soft feathers of white like a blanket covering the ground

Snow flakes like a ballet of beauty silent dancers not making a sound.

It kept falling down getting deeper and deeper I thought when will it cease.

I knew there was no way I could make it stop soon it was up to my knees.

Who needs snow I grumbled to myself its a trouble and nuisance to

All of a sudden I heard the soft voice of the Lord saying "Who needs this snow you do."

Without rain or snow what would the Farmers do without any moisture in the soil.

The seeds that were sown couldn't push through dry ground so their labor would be a futile toil

So the next time it snows dont whine or complain just accept the

snowy day.
   Get out the old snow shovel put a Smile on your face and shovel shovel away.
   The Waterview Church Smile Greeters respect those snow showers to.
   Their Smiles will melt the snow from your path and let Gods Love shine through.
      Our Love and a Smile ☺
      Hattie D + Nina

www.ingramcontent.com/pod-product-compliance
Lightning Source LLC
Chambersburg PA
CBHW040054100426
42734CB00043B/3266